Messerschmitt Me 210/410

in action

By George Punka

Color By Don Greer
& Tom Tullis

Illustrated by Joe Sewell
& Lori Basham

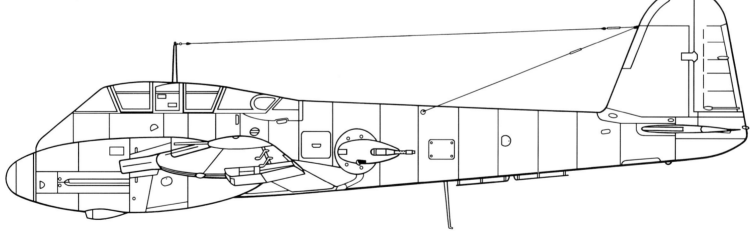

Aircraft Number 1148

squadron/signal publications

A pair of Me 410s of I./ZG 26 are attacked by P-51 Mustangs of the 328th Fighter Squadron, 352nd Fighter Group, 8th Air Force during late 1944. In air-to-air combat, the Me 410, like the earlier Bf 110 and Me 210, was at a disadvantage against the faster, more maneuverable single engine fighters.

If you have any photographs of aircraft, armor, soldiers or ships of any nation, particularly wartime snapshots, why not share them with us and help make Squadron/Signal's books all the more interesting and complete in the future. Any photograph sent to us will be copied and the original returned. The donor will be fully credited for any photos used. Please send them to:

Squadron/Signal Publications, Inc.
1115 Crowley Drive
Carrollton, TX 75011-5010

Acknowledgements

A special, Thanks, Danke scheön and Köszönöm, to the following persons and organizations for their assistance with photographs and information on the Me 210/410:

József Bilau	Rick Chapmann
Béla Csapo	Hans Peter Dabrowski
Joachim Dressel	Robert Gretzyngier
Manfred Griehl	István Gazsi
Christlieb Fenger	Kálmán Hary
László Jávor	Oszkár Kalmár
Ferenc Kovács	Lajos Kovács
Dr.Volker Koos	Viktor Kulikov
Walter Matthiesen	Theodor Mohr
Heinz J. Nowarra	János Péterdy
Peter Petrick	Willy Radinger
Christoph Regels	Matti Salonen
Gyula Sárhidai	László Schmidt
Hans-Heiri Stapfer	Márton Szabó
Károly Wágner	Hannes Wenko
Prof. Dr. Hans-Armin Weirich	Günther Wiesinger
László Winkler	Kálmán Wittinger
Fritz Trenkle	Helmut Zittier
Aero História	Archiv Kruse
Archieves Lorant	Hadtörténeti Intézet/Budapest
International War Museum	Kanadai Magyar Szárnyak
Newark Air Museum	USAF
Royal Danish Air Force	Smithsonian Institute

Dedication

I have to thank three persons for this work: Lieutenant Hannes Wenko, who encouraged me to write the history of the Me 410, Mr. Peter Petrick, who placed his fantastic photographic collection at my disposal and Sergeant Oszkár Kalmár, who gave me the first photos of a Hungarian Me 210.

Additionally, I received invaluable help from former pilots of ZG 1 and ABKZ-Ungarn. A number of former Me 210/410 pilots attended the meeting of Veteran Flyers, held during September of 1992 in Hungary. During this meeting they met many of their former enemies, American and Soviet flyers.

At the reunion, they recalled memories of the fights and their youth, which hate had stolen many years. Let us think about them when reading this book and think about our unquiet world. It is up to us to see that these dark days of history are never repeated.

I am Hungarian, so according to Hungarian customs, let us have a drink after publication of the book. A drink to the health of both former and present flyers: Cheers! Zum Wohl! Egészségünkre!

A Me 410A-1 (GH+YG) enroute to its target during October of 1944. The aircraft was assigned to I./KG 51 at Hörsching, Austria. (Matthiesen)

3

Introduction

The planning for what would become the Me 210, began during 1937, when the Messerschmitt design team began work on a new heavy fighter-bomber to replace the Bf 110 which had revealed a number of shortcomings. The design, as envisioned by the *Reichsluftfahrtministerium*, or R.L.M., was to have been an improved version of the Bf 110, capable of undertaking the roles of heavy "destroyer", reconnaissance and dive-bomber, with more powerful engines and increased fire-power. Construction of the prototype was initiated during 1938 and the first aircraft, the Me 210 V1 (radio code D-AABF, Werk Nr. 2100001), made its first flight on 2 September 1939.

The Me 210V-1 was a low-wing cantilever monoplane, with twin vertical tail surfaces, very similar to the earlier Bf 110. The fuselage profile; however, differed markedly from the earlier fighter. The new aircraft had a very blunt nose and a squat fuselage with a bubble type canopy for the pilot and radio-operator.

It was powered with two 1,050 hp Daimler-Benz DB 601A-1 liquid-cooled engines. After the first test flights, the test pilot, Dr. Ing. Hermann Wurster, reported that the new aircraft possessed very bad flying characteristics, with poor lateral and longitudinal stability.

The second prototype, the Me 210V-2 (radio code WL-ABEO, Werk Nr. 2100002) was modified and fitted with a single fin and rudder. The second prototype also differed from its predecessor in having a cockpit canopy with bulged side windows and mock-ups of the remote controlled, rear-firing machine gun turrets on each side of the fuselage. Each turret was to contain a 13MM MG 131 machine gun. The aircraft also had the outer wing-panels of the Me 210V-3, which were swept back some five degrees and wing mounted dive brakes. Even with these changes, the aircraft was still extremely unstable and eventually crashed on 5 September 1940, while on a flight to conduct flutter tests with *Flugkapitän* Fritz Wendel at the controls. The V-3 prototype's fuselage was assigned static test role.

The V-4 prototype (radio code CF+BB, Werk Nr. 2100004) was the first of some fifteen *Versuchs* (experimental) machines, each being assigned to test modifications, equipment installations and the items of equipment themselves. The remaining thirteen prototypes were completed during the Spring and early Summer of 1941.

The Me 210V-5 and V-9 were used to test wing modifications, the V-6, V-10 and V-11 were used to test general flight handling characteristics and the V-7 and V-8 were used to test de-icing and landing gear modifications. The Me 210V-12 had experimental dive brakes and

was used for dive bombing trials. The V-13 was fitted with a four blade propeller and was used for comparison trials with aircraft equipped with three blade units. The V-14 was fitted with an anti-spin parachute and was used for spinning trials. The V-15 was used to test various items of radio equipment and the final prototype, the V-16, was intended for de-icing trials.

As it finally emerged, the Messerschmitt Me 210 was a twin-engine, low wing, all metal, two-seat monoplane fighter. The wings were of all metal construction and were built in three pieces, two outer wing panels and a wing center section. The wings had slat-type dive-brakes fitted above and below the outer wings, just outboard of the engine nacelles, and behind the wing main spars. These air brakes were hydraulically operated. The ailerons were fabric covered.

The fuselage was a light alloy monocoque structure with a single vertical stabilizer. The rudders and elevators were also fabric covered. The cockpit for the pilot and radio-operator gunner was covered with a bubble type canopy with bulged sides and an armor glass windshield.

The undercarriage retracted rearward, with the main landing gear wheels resting in bays within the engine nacelles and being fully enclosed by hinged doors on the rear of the nacelles. The tail wheel was also fully retractable, retracting into a bay in the rear portion of the fuselage. The aircraft was powered by two 1,050 hp Daimler-Benz DB-610 engines driving hydraulically operated V.D.M. three-bladed, constant speed, all metal propellers.

Armament specified for the Me 210 consisted of two 20MM MG 151 cannons with 350 rounds each and two 7.9MM MG 17 guns with 1,000 rounds, firing from the extreme nose and two 13MM MG 131 guns with 450 rounds in the remotely controlled gun blisters on either side of the fuselage. These guns were remotely fired by the radio-operator/gunner. A bomb bay

Messerschmitt's chief test pilot, Dr. Hermann Wurster, after the first flight of the Me 210V-1 (D-AABF) on 5 September 1939. Dr. Wurster reported that the prototype suffered from poor lateral stability and had generally poor flight characteristics. (Mohr)

The Me 210V-1 prototype had twin vertical stabilizers, similar to those used on the earlier Bf 110. The port propeller is feathered, indicating that the aircraft had an engine problem in flight. (Mohr)

under the extreme nose had provisions for carrying either eight 110 pound, two 551 pound or two 1,102 pound bombs.

Even while the various flight tests and trials were still going on, the *Reichsluftfahrtministerium* placed a production order for 1,000 Me 210As and the first pre-production variant, the Me 210A-0 began leaving the assembly lines during 1940. The first pre-production Me 210A-0 reached the Luftwaffe special test unit, *Erprobungsgruppe* 210, just before the end of 1940.

The port side of the DB 601F engine installed in the Me 210V-1 prototype. This engine produced 1,050 hp and drove a three blade VDM propeller. The landing gear is fully extended with the oleo strut at the full down position. (Radinger)

The Messerschmitt Me 210 program was plagued with accidents. The Me 210V-10 prototype (GI+SN Werk Nr. 010) ended up on its belly after the landing gear failed on landing after a test flight on 16 June 1941. (Mohr)

The Me 210V-13 was modified to test an electric de-icing system and the automatic radiator cooler flaps. It was also outfitted with a four blade propeller to run comparison tests against other prototypes fitted with three blade units. (Mohr)

Later, the Me 210V-13 prototype, GI+SQ, also suffered a landing gear failure after making an emergency power-off landing on 31 May 1941. The V-13 was the only prototype fitted with a four blade propeller. (Mohr)

Development

Me 210V-1

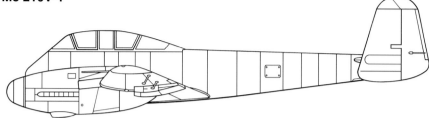

Me 210A-1/U

Me 210V-3

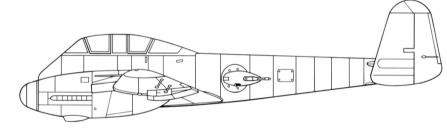

Me 210Ca-1

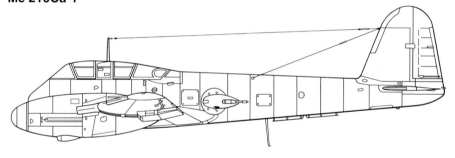

Me 210A-0

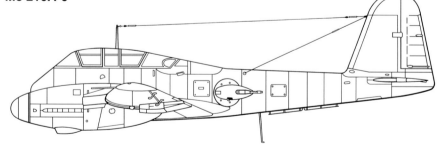

Me 410A-1

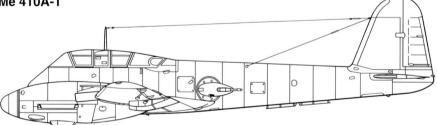

Me 210A Series

Me 210A-0

By the late Spring of 1941, both the Augsburg and Regensburg factories had initiated assembly of the Me 210A-0 pre-production series (which would come to include some ninety-four aircraft), with the first aircraft rolling out during April.

The Me 210A-0 was basically identical to the late prototypes, with the exception of the engines. The Me 210A-0 utilized 1,305 hp Daimler-Benz DB-601F liquid-cooled engines in place of the earlier 1,050 hp DB-601A-1 engines.

The Me 210 was intended to be a heavy fighter with a secondary capability as a fighter-bomber/dive bomber. A comprehensive service evaluation of the Me 210A-0 was begun during late 1941 and it was found that the earlier prototypes were too few in number to complete all the testing needed. As a result, eight Me 210A-0s were sent to join the test program. Five Me 210A-0s were also modified by Blohm & Voss as dual control trainers to aid in the pilot conversion program. By the end of 1941, it had been determined that the Me 210A-0 had too many shortcomings, particularly in stability, for it to be a suitable combat aircraft. Despite this evaluation, production was to continue and two additional variants, the Me 210A-1 and Me 210A-2 were ordered into production.

One Me 210A-0 (NE+BH, Werk Nr.101) was modified with a lengthened rear fuselage, being redesignated the Me 210V-17 on 14 March 1942. A comparison between this aircraft and the Me 210V-16 left little doubt that the modification had a positive effect on the aircraft's handling qualities. In July of 1942, another Me 210A-0 aircraft was fitted with wing leading edge slots. This modification was found to drastically improve the aircraft's characteristics in a slide slip and these slats were ordered to be retrofitted to all Me 210s.

Early production Me 210 fuselages rest on four wheel dollies in the Messerschmitt work shop. These aircraft were fitted with the early style cockpit canopy. While the side turret mounts are in place, the 13MM guns have not been mounted. (Mohr)

Ground crewmen prepare a Me 210A-1 (VN+AD, Werk Nr. 0166) for its acceptance test flight on the Messerschmitt flight line. This aircraft has the bulged canopy, and the wing mounted speed brakes are in the open position. (Radinger)

Thirty-seven early production Me 210 fuselages line either side of the assembly hall during 1942. (Radinger)

Fuselage Development

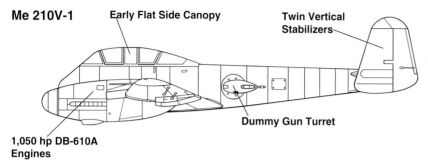

Me 210V-1

Early Flat Side Canopy

Twin Vertical Stabilizers

1,050 hp DB-610A Engines

Dummy Gun Turret

Me 210A-0

Bulged Canopy

Single Fin And Rudder

Antenna Post

1,350 hp DB-601F Engine

13MM MG 131 Machine Gun Turret (Each Side)

Factory fresh Me 210A-0s line the airfield at the Messerschmitt works in Augsburg. The aircraft in the middle was coded GT+VZ. These aircraft had the short fuselage common to all early production Me 210s. (Radinger)

Me 210A-1

The first Me 210A-1 heavy fighter rolled out in November of 1941. The Me 210 A-1 carried a forward-firing armament of two 20MM MG 151 cannons and two 7.9MM MG 17 machine guns in the nose and two 13MM MG 131 weapons in the FDL 131 fuselage side gun positions.

Me 210A-2

The Me 210A-2 was a fighter-bomber variant of the Me 210 and was similar to the Me 210A-1 except for the bomb load. The Me 210 A-2 was essentially a dive-bomber with a limited heavy fighter capability, It carried an internal bomb load of one 2,204 pound (1,000 kg) PC 1000RS bomb or two 1,102 pound (500kg SD 500) bombs, or two 551 pound (250kg SC 250) bombs or eight 110 pound (50kg SC 50) bombs. This bomb load was augmented by four 110 pound (50kg SC 50s) bombs on under wing racks mounted under the wing center section.

During April of 1942, front line units equipped with the Me 210 were suffering an unacceptable accident rate and both Messerschmitt workshops, Augsburg and the MIAG at Braunschweig were ordered to halt Me 210 production and a commission was established to investigate the program. Apart from the *Versuchs* (test) aircraft, some ninety-four Me 210A-0s and ninety Me 210A-1 versions had left the assembly lines, while a further 370 were in various stages of construction. In addition, materials and main components had been prepared for an additional 800 machines.

Tests had revealed that the lengthened fuselage and wing slats cured most of the poor handling problems with the Me 210 and production was started once again, with the intent to rebuild existing Me 210A-1s and Me 210A-2s with the new fuselage and to complete those aircraft that had been near completion at the time of production termination. In 1942 some ninety-five aircraft were delivered, followed by eighty-nine in 1943 and seventy-four in 1944. Most of these later aircraft did not reach front-line units and many were disassembled to provide parts for Me 410s then entering production.

Electricians work on a Me 210A-1 outside the Messerschmitt works. The upper canopy radio mast has been removed and the gun turrets are covered to protect them from the weather. (Trenkle)

Engine Nacelle Development

Me 210V-1

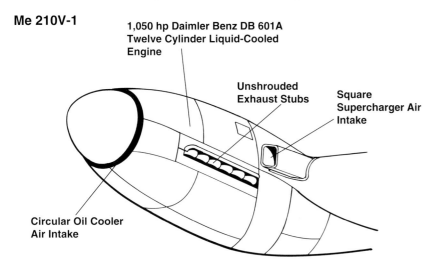

1,050 hp Daimler Benz DB 601A Twelve Cylinder Liquid-Cooled Engine

Unshrouded Exhaust Stubs

Square Supercharger Air Intake

Circular Oil Cooler Air Intake

Me 210A-1

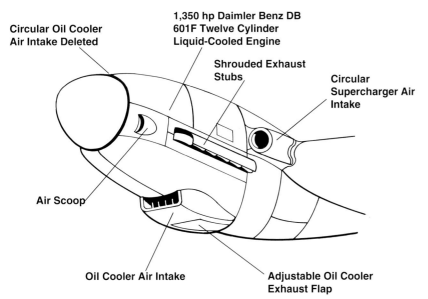

1,350 hp Daimler Benz DB 601F Twelve Cylinder Liquid-Cooled Engine

Circular Oil Cooler Air Intake Deleted

Shrouded Exhaust Stubs

Circular Supercharger Air Intake

Air Scoop

Oil Cooler Air Intake

Adjustable Oil Cooler Exhaust Flap

This Me 210A-1 (PN+PF, Werk Nr.107) had the starboard landing gear leg fail on landing. The crew of two was housed under a bubble type canopy, with the radio-operator/gunner facing the rear. (Mohr)

A pair of Me 210A-1s of 3./SKG 210 in training flight during January of 1942. The aircraft in the foreground (S9+IL, Werk Nr.2261) was later damaged in a crash landing. (Petrick)

This Me 210A-1 (DU+IB, Werk Nr. 032) has a modified cockpit canopy. The aircraft carried the Werk Number on the lower fin in White. (Radinger)

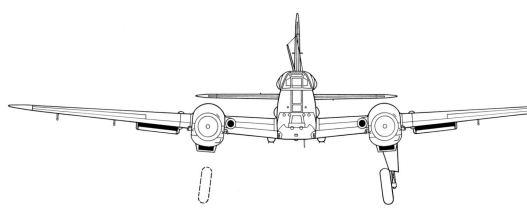

Specification

Messerschmitt Me 210A-0

Wingspan..53 feet 71/3 inches (16.3(m)
Length..36 feet 7 3/4 inches (12 m)
Height..14 feet .5 inches (4.2 m)
Empty Weight.......................................15,586 pounds (7,069 kg)
Maximum Weight..................................21,397 pounds (9,705 kg)

Powerplant...Two 1,350 hp Daimler Benz DB 601F
                                               Twelve Cylinder liquid cooled engines
Armament...Two forward firing 7.9ᴍᴍ MG 17
                                               machine guns and two 20ᴍᴍ MG 151
                                               cannons and two 13ᴍᴍ MG 131 machine guns
                                               in rear firing remote controlled turrets. Up to 2,204
                                               pounds of bombs.
Speed...288 mph (463.4 kph)
Service Ceiling.....................................29,200 feet (8,900 m)
Range...1,130 miles (1,818 km)
Crew...Two

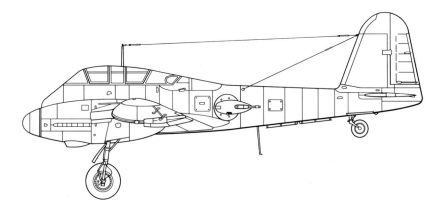

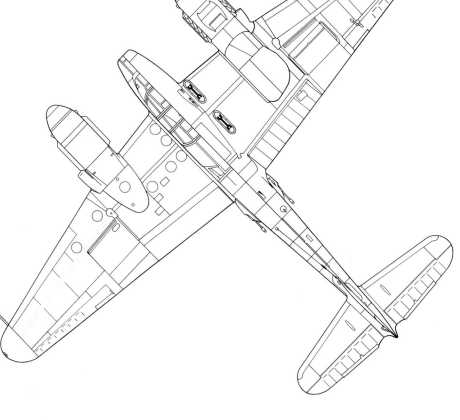

Me 210B

The Me 210B (B-0 /B-1) was a high-speed photographic reconnaissance version of the Me 210A-1. The aircraft differed from the fighter in that the forward firing armament was reduced by the removal of the two 7.9MM machine guns, leaving only two 20MM MG 151 cannons. Two cameras, either Rb 75/30s, Rb 50/30s or Rb 20/30s aerial reconnaissance cameras were mounted in the bomb bay. The machines were also fitted with two 237 gallon (900 liter) auxiliary fuel tanks.

Two Me 210A-1s were converted as pre-production Me 210B-0s, but only two production Me 210B-1 aircraft were completed before Me 210 production was terminated. No further reconnaissance variants were produced once production resumed.

There were a number of projected variants of the Me 210 that were not built, including the Me 210C-1, C-2 and D-1, which were to be powered by DB 605B engines with MW 1 Methanol injection. These aircraft were modifications of Me 210A-1s, A-2s and B-1s. The D-1 and Da-1 reconnaissance aircraft were to carry only the forward-firing MG 151s and the two MG 131 turret guns for the radio operator-gunner. The bomb bay was modified to hold one RB 20-RB 50 camera or two RB 75-RB 50 cameras.

Other projected variants include the Me 210E-1, F-1 and F-2 (basically Me 210As with Daimler Benz 603 engines, and a ground attack variant known as the Me 210S-1 which was similar to the A-1 but with heavy armor protection for the cabin, bomb bay, engines and the oil coolers. The last design, the Me 210S-2 was a Me 210S-1 with DB 605 engines.

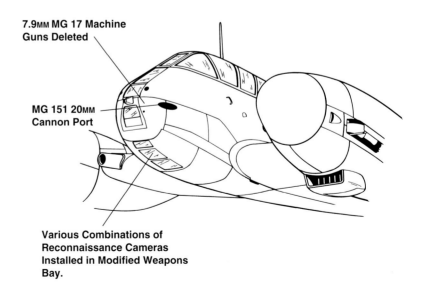

This Me 210A forward fuselage was used as a test bed for testing the 210MM RZ 100 rocket weapon intended to be used on the Me 410. (Radinger)

Me 210A-1

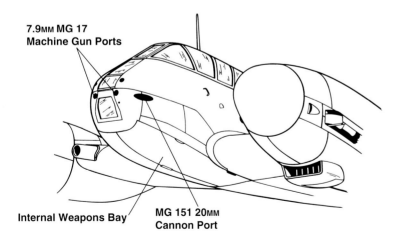

7.9MM MG 17 Machine Gun Ports

Internal Weapons Bay

MG 151 20MM Cannon Port

Me 210B/B-1/Da-1

7.9MM MG 17 Machine Guns Deleted

MG 151 20MM Cannon Port

Various Combinations of Reconnaissance Cameras Installed in Modified Weapons Bay.

Me 210 in German Service

The first Me 210A-0s left the assembly lines in early 1940 and were delivered to *Erprobungsgruppe 210*. This unit had been formed in July of 1940 with the assigned task of conducting operational testing the Me 210 and developing combat tactics for the fighter-bomber. Initially equipped with a number of Bf 109s and Bf 110s while waiting for delivery of the Me 210s, the unit commenced operations over England in the Summer of 1940. The first leader of the *Gruppe* was *Hauptmann* Walter Rubensdörffer, who was killed, along with his radio-operator/gunner, while flying a Bf 110 on a mission over England.

Until the Summer of 1941, *Erprobungsgruppe 210* was the only Luftwaffe unit flying the Me 210 and its reports on the flight characteristics of the new fighter were far from complementary. At this same time the unit lost another key leader, *Oberleutnant* (First Lieutenant) Heinz Forgatsch, of *3./SKG 210* who was killed at Rechlin on 23 September 1941 while testing a Me 210.

Even so, the Luftwaffe issued the Me 210A-1 to *II./Zerstorergeschwader 1* during the Winter of 1941/42. The unit, deployed on the Eastern Front was re-equipped with the new aircraft, but, after a short period of operations, the unit again re-equipped, this time with Bf 110s.

After the Me 210 was put through a series of modifications, the rebuilt Me 210A-1s were issued to a special experimental unit, designated *Versuchsstaffel 210*, which achieved operational status during August of 1942, based at Soesterburg in central Holland. Once the unit had become operational under *Luftflotte 3*, its designator was changed to *16./KG 6*. The debut of the Me 210A-1 over Britain was inauspicious. On 6 September, two Me 210A-1s

This Me 210A-1 (SI+IX, Werk Nr. 0258) was involved in a landing accident with an Italian Savoia-Marchetti S.M. 84 at Lecce during January of 1943. The fuselage band is in White as are the crosses on the fuselage and the Werk Number on the fin. (Petrick)

A Me 210 A-1 (2H+IA) of Versuchsstaffel 210 during September of 1943. It is believed that the individual code letter (I) was probably painted Red. (Dressel)

were lost to RAF Typhoons over Yorkshire. The first crew, flying 2H+HA (Werk Nr. 2321) were wounded and captured, but the second aircraft, 2N+CA, was destroyed and both crewmen were killed.

A small number of modified Me 210A-1s had been delivered to *II./ZG 1* in Sicily. This unit operated with Bf 110s and Me 210s under *Fliegerführer Afrika*, protecting the *Afrika Korps* in Tunisia during early 1943. This unit had several losses in air battles over the coast of North Africa, with 2N+GS (Werk Nr.0036) being shot down and its crew, *Oberleutnant* Heinz Redlich, commandant of *III Gruppe* and his crewman *Feldwebel* (Sergeant) Friedrich Hamburger, being killed in action near Apollonia.

10./ZG 26 also received the Me 210 A-1 in Tunisia during early 1943. Their use of the Me 210 was short lived and by March, the squadron had converted to the Junkers Ju 88. In January of 1943, *2.(F)/122* and *Stab of FAGr.122*, operated a mixed unit of Me 210s and Ju 88s. These reconnaissance units soon discarded the Me 210s, and became fully equipped with Ju 88s.

These Me 210A-2s were used in the *Schnellbomber* (fast bomber) role by III./ZG 1 in Sicily during 1942. (Petrick)

A Me 210A-1 of ZG 1 at Trapani, North Africa during late 1942. The individual aircraft identification letter, F, is in White with a thin Red outline. (Petrick)

After many combat losses and other non-combat accidents, the Me 210s of *II.* and *III./ZG 1*, *I.* and *II./NJG 1* and several reconnaissance squadrons, were slowly replaced by Me 410s as they became more available.

Luftwaffe units equipped with Me 210 aircraft during 1941-1943 included: *Erprobungsgruppe 210*, *I./SKG 210* (S9+), *Ergänzung-Zerstörer Gruppe* (4H+), *Versuchsstaffel 210* (*16./KG 6*, 2H+), *III./ZG 1* (2N+),*2.(F)/122* (F6+), *10./ZG 26* (3U+), *KG 51* (9K+), *V./KG 2* (U5+), *KG 101/KSG 1* (5T+), *NJG 101* (9W+), *1.(F)/121* (7A+), *I./NJG 1* (G9+), *ZG 101* (6U+[probably]), *FUG 1*, and *Luftbeobachtung Staffel 3*.

Many other Me 210s were used as trainers for units working up on the Messerschmitt Me 410.

Ground crewmen work on a Me 210A-1 (2N+FR) of 7./ZG 1 on a desert field in North Africa. The starboard propeller spinner was in two colors while the port propeller spinner was in White, with the aircraft's individual code letter, F, painted in Black. (Petrick)

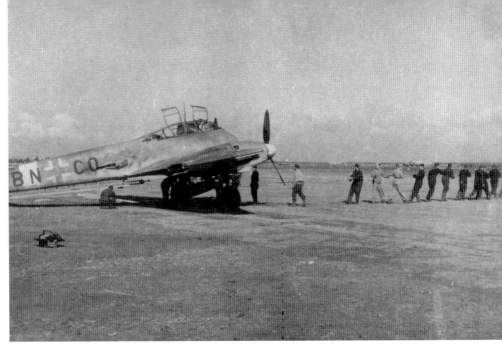

Ground crewmen haul on the ropes used to lift a bomb into the bomb bay of this Me 210A-1(BN+CO, Werk Nr. 229) of III./ZG 1 at Lecce during 1942. The fuselage cross was Light Gray with a White outline. (Petrick)

A driver picks up the pilot and radio-operator/gunner of a Me 210A-1 of III./ZG 1 after a mission during November of 1942. This aircraft has unusually painted propeller spinners, each side being painted different. (Petrick)

13

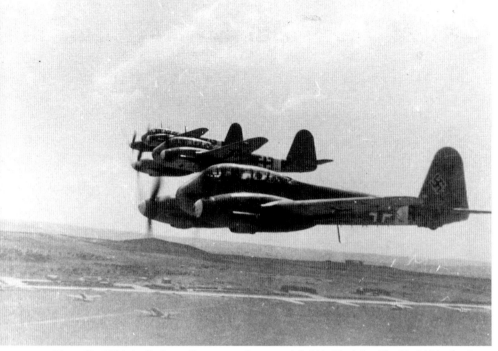

Three Me 210A-1s fly formation over a German airfield in Tunisia. The Me 210 in the foreground (2N+JR) has the individual aircraft letter J in White with a thin Red outline against a White band fuselage band. (Petrick)

A Me 210A of 8./ZG parked on the field at Catania, Sicily. This aircraft has a replacement rudder that does not match the rest of the aircraft's camouflage. The A in the radio code is in Red. (Petrick)

This Me 210A-1 (2N+AT, Werk Nr. 039) made a forced landing at Castelli on 8 November 1942. The aircraft had the A of the radio code in Yellow and the Werk Number on the vertical fin was in White. Crewmen have already begun to remove panels from the aircraft. (Petrick)

A pair of Me 210s of 7./ZG 1 on patrol over Tunisia, North Africa during 1942. The lead aircraft (2N+BR) has the individual aircraft letter, B, in White, while the unit code letters (2N) are in small Black letters on the White fuselage band. (Petrick)

This Me 210A-1 (2N+AS) on the landing ground at Catania, Sicily during late 1942 had the propeller spinners in Blue (Petrick)

(Right) It took a lot of muscle to load the bomb bay of this Me 210A-1 (GT+VJ, Werk Nr. 092) with two 1,102 pound bombs. The block and tackle rig was secured to the tail wheel, with the line running out to the front of the aircraft. Once all was in place, ground crews hauled on the line until the bombs were secured on the racks. Later this aircraft was recoded as 2N+JT and while carrying this code, it crashed. The propeller spinners were painted Red and Black. (Petrick)

A ground crewman sets up the block and tackle used to raise the loaded bomb rack into the bomb bay of a Me 210A-1 in North Africa, while another crewman holds 20mm cannon rounds. The internal bomb bay of the Me 210 could hold up to 2,200 pounds of bombs, in various combinations of weapons. Common loads were eight 110 pound bombs, two 551 pound bombs or two 1,102 pound weapons. (Dressel)

The gun turret cover has been removed so that armament crews can load belted 13mm ammunition into the starboard MG 131 gun turret on this Me 210A-1, while other crewmen prepare to load the bomb bay. Other mechanics are servicing the cockpit, making sure that all is in readiness for the aircraft's next mission. (Petrick)

The pilot of this Me 210A-1 (KD+JL, Werk Nr. 220) confers with other officers after returning from a mission at Lecce during January of 1943. The aircraft appears to have suffered some battle damage to the rear fuselage next to the fuselage cross. (Petrick)

This Me 210A-1 (2N+LT, Werk Nr. 205) ran off the runway at Lecce airfield and crashed into this stone wall because of brake failure on 4 March 1943. The code letter, L, was in Yellow. (Petrick)

A Me 210A-1 of 2./(F)122 made a belly landing at Chenisia on 25 March 1943. Ground crewmen had painted over the White markings on this aircraft with Gray paint to prevent the enemy from using the highly visible White markings as aiming points. (Petrick)

F6 WK was repaired and put back into service. Ground crewmen are working on the wing prior to replacing it on the repaired fuselage. The aircraft's markings appear to have been repainted. The aircraft in the background is a Bf 109. (Petrick)

This Me 210 (DI+NF, Werk Nr. 0194) has an L 10 glider and LT 950 torpedo mounted under the fuselage at the Luftwaffe test base at Gotenhafen, Hexengrund, during June of 1942. (Nowarra)

One Me 210A-2 (Werk Nr. 2350), powered by DB601F engines, was delivered to Japan under the Nippon-German Technical Exchange Agreement for evaluation during January of 1943. The aircraft was flown in standard Luftwaffe camouflage with the German markings replaced by Japanese markings. Unlike other German aircraft that were sent to Japan, the Allies did not assign a code name to the Me 210. (Nowarra)

The crew of a Me 210A-1 of 2./(F)122 are congratulated on completing a milestone in the unit's history, while based in Italy. Usually such ceremonies were conducted after completion of a certain number of sorties, such as the 500th or 1,000th. The text on the engine reads: *Hier nicht öffnen* (No open here).

Messerschmitt Me 210Ca-1

Under the German-Hungarian Mutual Armament Program, which had been finalized in June of 1941 for the production of Bf 109, Me 210 (later Me 410), Junkers Ju 52 and Arado Ar 96, the *Dunai Repülögépgyár* (Danube Aircraft Factory) at Horthyliget was established for the license manufacture of both engines and airframes. The factory was provided with all the necessary machine-tools and jigs needed to begin production directly from Messerschmitt.

One Me 210 A-0 (radio code PN+PD, Werk Nr. 2100105) was re-engined with 1,475 hp DB 605B engines without MW 1 Methanol injection. This aircraft served as a pattern aircraft for the Me 210 and was fitted with the lengthened fuselage and wing leading edge slots. The aircraft was to be built in two variants, the Me 210C-1 and Me 210Ca-1 (roughly equal to the Me 210A-1 and Me 210A-2). Other than the engines, the Hungarian produced variants were the same as the modified Me 210As being assembled by Messerschmitt.

The first Hungarian Me 210Ca-1 (radio code RF+PA, Werk Nr. 210001) made its first test flight on 21 December 1942, with test pilot Captain Dénes Eszenyi at the controls. After a series of successful test flights the *Honvédelmi Minisztérium* (Ministry of National Defense) ordered the Me 210 into production with a short production of five machines.

The German-Hungarian Committee concluded an agreement under which the Hungarian factory would produce 557 Messerschmitt Me 210s and 817 Me 410B-1s, with two thirds of all Hungarian produced aircraft going to the Luftwaffe. The first three Me 210Ca-1a (RF+PA, RF+PB, Werk Nr. 210003 and RF+PC, Werk Nr. 210005) were accepted by the Luftwaffe in April of 1943.

The Royal Hungarian *Honvéd* Air Force received its first two aircraft from the production line (ZO+01 and ZO+02) in July of 1943 and by the end of that year, some 100 Me 210Ca-1s had been built, including two that were modified for long-range reconnaissance (ZO+06, Werk Nr. 210.013006 and ZO+07, Werk Nr. 210.014007).

By 1 April 1944, the Danube Air Factory had produced a total of 176 aircraft; however, the intended production of the Me 410 was cancelled because many of the promised tools and jigs did not arrive from Germany.

A Hungarian pilot describes the performance and weapons of a factory fresh Me 210Ca-1 (ZO+32, Werk Nr. 210.074032) to new crews on the airfield at Kecskemet during 1944. (Javor)

On 3 and 13 April 1944, heavy USAAF bombing attacks damaged a total of fifty-nine aircraft on the airfield and in the factory. As a result of the damage to the Me 210 line, the factory shifted production to the Bf 109. Before production ceased, a number of Me 210 aircraft that had been far along in their production cycle were completed and handed over for flight testing. Total production was 270 aircraft, of which 110 were transferred to Luftwaffe units.

One of the projects undertaken by the Hungarian factory was the modification of one Me 210Ca-1 into an assault aircraft for use against American bombers. The aircraft (code ZO+O3, Werk Nr. 210.007.003) was modified in March of 1944, with the project being completed in July of 1944. The MG 17 machine guns were deleted and a single 40mm 39M type anti-aircraft cannon was installed in the lower portion of the nose. Additionally, three 150mm *Nebelwerfer* rocket-tubes were mounted under each wing outboard panel. Firing trials took place on 24 October 1944 after many delays due to American bombing raids. After a successful series of tests , it was decided to modify thirty aircraft, but only four were actually finished.

This early production Hungarian-built Me 210 (ZO+06) was later modified into a reconnaissance aircraft under the designation Me 210Da. The aircraft carries the Black and White Hungarian cross on the wings and fuselage and Red/White/Green bands on the fin and horizontal stabilizers. (Winkler)

This Hungarian Me 210Ca-1 was totally destroyed in a hangar at the *Dunai Repülögépgyár* (Danube Aircraft Factory) in Horthyliget after an American bombing raid on 3 April 1944. The bulges under the wing are ETC 50 bomb racks. (Punka)

Armament Development

Me 210Ca-1

17 7.9ᴍᴍ MG
Machine Gun Ports

Internal Weapons Bay

MG 151 20ᴍᴍ
Cannon Port

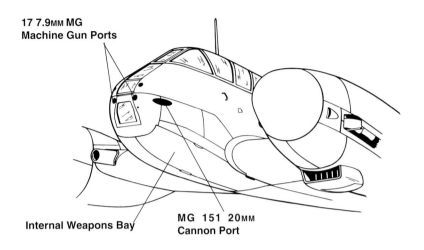

Me 210Ca-1 *Zerstörer*

MG 17 7.9ᴍᴍ Machine
Gun Ports

40ᴍᴍ 39M Anti-Aircraft
Cannon

MG 151 20ᴍᴍ Cannon Port

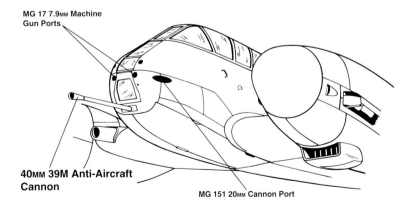

This Me 210 was modified with a 40ᴍᴍ 39M anti-aircraft cannon for the *Zerstörer* role. Additionally, ZO+03 also carried three 150ᴍᴍ rocket tubes under each outer wing panel. The aircraft was based at Varpalota during October of 1944. It was decided to modify thirty aircraft to this configuration, but only four were actually finished. (Punka)

A Hungarian night fighter Me 210Ca-1 of 5/1. *Éjszakai Vadász Század* (night fighter squadron) after suffering a collapsed landing gear during the Summer of 1944. The squadron insignia, an Owl, was painted on the fuselage just behind the MG 151 cannon port on the nose. (Petrick)

19

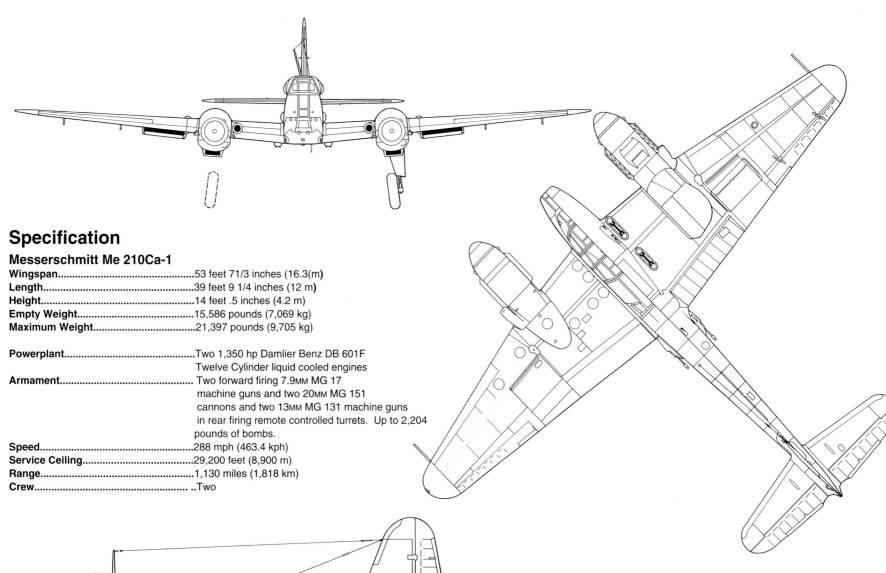

Specification

Messerschmitt Me 210Ca-1

Wingspan..53 feet 71/3 inches (16.3(m)
Length..39 feet 9 1/4 inches (12 m)
Height...14 feet .5 inches (4.2 m)
Empty Weight..15,586 pounds (7,069 kg)
Maximum Weight....................................21,397 pounds (9,705 kg)

Powerplant...Two 1,350 hp Damlier Benz DB 601F
　　　　　　　　　　　　　　　　　　　　　Twelve Cylinder liquid cooled engines
Armament...Two forward firing 7.9ᴍᴍ MG 17
　　　　　　　　　　　　　　　　　　　　　machine guns and two 20ᴍᴍ MG 151
　　　　　　　　　　　　　　　　　　　　　cannons and two 13ᴍᴍ MG 131 machine guns
　　　　　　　　　　　　　　　　　　　　　in rear firing remote controlled turrets. Up to 2,204
　　　　　　　　　　　　　　　　　　　　　pounds of bombs.
Speed...288 mph (463.4 kph)
Service Ceiling.......................................29,200 feet (8,900 m)
Range...1,130 miles (1,818 km)
Crew... ..Two

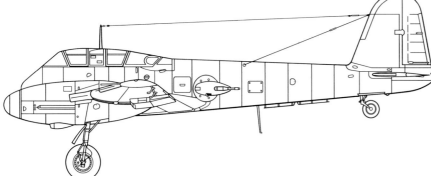

Me 210 In Hungarian Service

The first Hungarian unit which was formed with the Me 210, was the 5/1. Night Fighter Squadron, known as the *Bagoly* or Owl Squadron, based at Ferihegy, southeast of Budapest, the capital of Hungary. The squadron received its first aircraft in June of 1943, but the crews were not trained for the night fighting mission. The night fighter unit, commanded by *Százados* (Captain) Ádám Krúdy, had twelve aircraft and made its operational debut on 3 April 1944 against the day bomber formations of the USAAF's 15th Air Force. On this day they returned to base without results. Two days later *Örmester* (Sergeant) Dezsö Zsámboki shot down a B-24 Liberator of the 451st Bomb Group for the unit's first kill.

Shortly after the USAAF began bombing attacks against Hungarian cities, the commander of the Air Force Experimental Institute, *Alezredes* (Lieutenant Colonel) Loránt Dóczy formed a new destroyer squadron with the highly qualified test pilots and gunners assigned to the institute. This unit was known as the Air Force Experimental Institute Combat Squadron and it was equipped with eighteen Me 210Ca-1s.

On 12 April the unit was alerted of an incoming raid and took off with twelve aircraft to engage the American bombers, although they did not observe any of the attacking Liberators going down. After the engagement over Knin, Yugoslavia, one of the Me 210s (ZO+38) returned to base with a seriously wounded pilot, *Akadémikus* (Air Cadet) Sándor Hayden, who made a forced landing on Székesfehérvár airfield before dying of his wounds.

The next day, 13 April, the 15th Air Force again bombed targets in the area around Budapest and Györ. Both Me 210 units were alerted to intercept the bomber formations southeast of Budapest. The night fighter unit lost nine aircraft with three crews being killed. Additionally, many of the Me 210s were damaged in the engagement. The 5/1. Squadron claimed two P-38 and one B-24, but this was the last combat sortie for the unit with the Me 210.

This Me 210Ca-1 was flown by the squadron leader of 102.2 *Gyorsbombázó század,* (Fast Bomber Squadron, known as the Tiger Squadron during July of 1944. The unit was based at Hajdúdöszörmény, Hungary. (Punka)

The Air Force Experimental Institute Combat Squadron also suffered heavy losses. Four of the Me 210s were shot down by P-38 Lightnings, among them the aircraft flown by *Alezredes* Dóczy. During the fight his Me 210 (ZO+54) was observed by others in the unit as being on fire. The commander's gunner successfully bailed out, but Dóczy made a belly landing with a severely damaged aircraft. The unit shot down four Liberators and two P-38s during the battle, but afterward the Me 210 was restricted from further any action against American bomber formations over Hungary.

The third Me 210 unit in the Royal Hungarian *Honvéd* Air Force was established for light-bombing and the close-support role, under the designation 102/1. *Gyorsbombázó század* (fast-bomber squadron), known as the *Sas* or Eagle squadron. The unit was formed with twelve Me 210Ca-1s during early June of 1944. The unit was first based at Zamosc, Poland and later in Bilgoraj and Mielec. During August the fast-bombers moved to Hajdúböszörmény in eastern Hungary.

The fourth and last Me 210 unit was 102/2. *Gyorsbombázó század*, known as the Tiger squadron, also based at Hajdúböszörmény. On 21 August 1944, both squadrons lost a number of their aircraft to a USAAF bombing raid on the airfield.

After receiving replacement aircraft, the Hungarian fast-bombers began support operations against the advancing Soviet Army. The squadrons attacked the bridges on the Danube, military transports, Soviet tanks and armored cars.

The first combat action for 102/1. Squadron took place on 20 September 1944. The target was the rail yard at Chortkow, in the Soviet Union, which was bombed with all of the unit's aircraft. The target was attacked using dive bombing tactics from an altitude of 6,561 feet (2,000 meters). The Germans photographed the results a few hours later and stated that the rail yard was eighty percent destroyed.

In November, the squadron attacked railways in southeastern Hungary, but during this attack they were intercepted by Soviet fighters with some of the Me 210s returning to base seriously damaged, both from the fighters and from enemy ground fire.

102/2. Squadron took part in an important action on 7 August 1944. A single aircraft, piloted by *Zászlós* (Cornet) Béla Csapó, conducted a reconnaissance flight over Kolomea in the Soviet Union and dropped four 154 pound (70 kg) bombs on the railway station at Delatin. During this flight, the pilot recorded seeing fifty to sixty four-engined aircraft on the airfield south of the town, probably American bombers from the 95th or 390th Bomb Groups, which had flown a shuttle mission to the Trzebinia synthetic oil refinery and landed on a Soviet base in area of Mirgorod. The Hungarian fast-bomber squadron came back a few hours later with six Me 210s and, diving from 16,000 feet (5,000 meters), dive bombed the airfield. Bombing results were good and reportedly a number of the bombers were left in flames and destroyed.

By December, a third Me 210Ca-1 squadron had been established at the Air Force Experimental Institute. Known as *Viiiám* or Lightning Squadron, the establishment of this unit allowed the formation 102. *Gyorsbombázó osztály* (Group), with all three of the fast-bomber units. The group was based at Várpalota and the three squadrons flew, between August of 1944 and March of 1945, some 800 missions and shot down twenty to twenty-five Soviet aircraft. The group remained active until early 1945. At the end of March 1945, the unit had moved its aircraft to the airfield at Parndorf in Austria. Here, German troops destroyed the remaining Me 210s on the ground because there was no available fuel to evacuate the aircraft and keep them from falling into Soviet hands.

A Me 210Ca-1 night fighter of 5/1. Night Fighter Squadron, known as the *Bagoly,* or Owl Squadron, on its belly at Ferihegy airfield during the Summer of 1944. The squadron's Owl insignia is barely visible on the nose. From the position of the lower propeller blades and the fact that the upper blade is unbent, indicating that the engine was not running on impact. (Petrick)

Ground crews work on the side guns of this Me 210Ca-1 (ZO+98, Werk Nr. 196098) at Hajdúböszörmény during the Summer of 1944. The White areas of both the national insignia and of the vertical fin band have been overpainted with Gray to tone them down. (Punka)

German and Hungarian pilots and radio-operator/gunners were trained together at Ferihegy, Hungary on the Me 210Ca-1 during 1944. A total of some 110 Me 210Ca-1s were delivered from Hungarian production lines to Luftwaffe units. (Weirich)

Hungarian fast-bomber pilot Örmester (Sergeant) Kalmar sitting on the port propeller spinner of a Me 210Ca-1, which was painted in RLM Gray-Black with a White spiral design on the tip. (Punka)

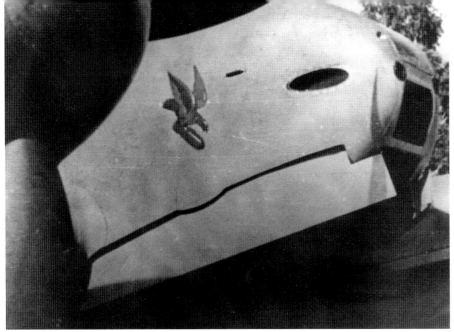

The diving eagle squadron insignia of 102/1. *Gyorsbombázó század* (Fast Bomber Squadron) was carried on the nose of its Me 210Ca-1s just behind the gun port for the MG 151 cannon and just above the open weapons bay door. (Kovács)

A new production Me 210Ca-1 parked on the grass on a forward airfield. The aircraft had large Black and White Hungarian insignia on the wing undersurfaces. The Me 210Ca-1 remained in production in Hungary until April of 1944, when American bombers destroyed most of the factory. (Kovács)

This Me 210Ca-1 of 102/2. *Gyorsbombázó század*, (Fast Bomber Squadron) at Hajdúböszörmény during the Summer of 1944 has had the nose-mounted weapons removed to lighten the aircraft for use in the reconnaissance role. (Punka)

Rear gunner and radio-operator Gazsi in the cockpit of a Hungarian Air Force Me 210Ca-1. Just above his left hand is the reflector gun sight for the two 13MM MG 131 turret guns while his right hand holds the pistol grip that controls the turret's movement. This pistol grip also had the gun firing trigger. (Punka)

A Hungarian Air Force radio-operator/gunner, dressed in leather winter flying clothes, poses in front of the 13mm gun turret on his Me 210Ca-1, ZO+67. The 7 is presented in the European slashed number style. (Punka)

Hadnagy (Lieutenant) Wágner and his radio/operator-gunner, Poos deplane after a successful action during August of 1944. The Black lines on the inside of the canopy are used to determine proper diving angles for dive bombing missions. (Wagner)

This Me 210Ca-1 (ZO+20) carried an experimental camouflage during the late Summer of 1944. The original Gray camouflage colors were overpainted with RLM Dark Green 82. (Jávor)

A ground crewman points to the shell hole in this Me 210Ca-1 of the 102/2. Squadron after a bombing mission in western Hungary. The spinner has a hand-painted White spiral and the unit's Tiger insignia is carried on the nose just to the rear of the cannon port. The Me 210Ca-1 carried four ETC 50 bomb racks under the wing root, which are visible just behind the open weapons bay doors. (Punka)

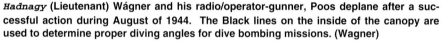

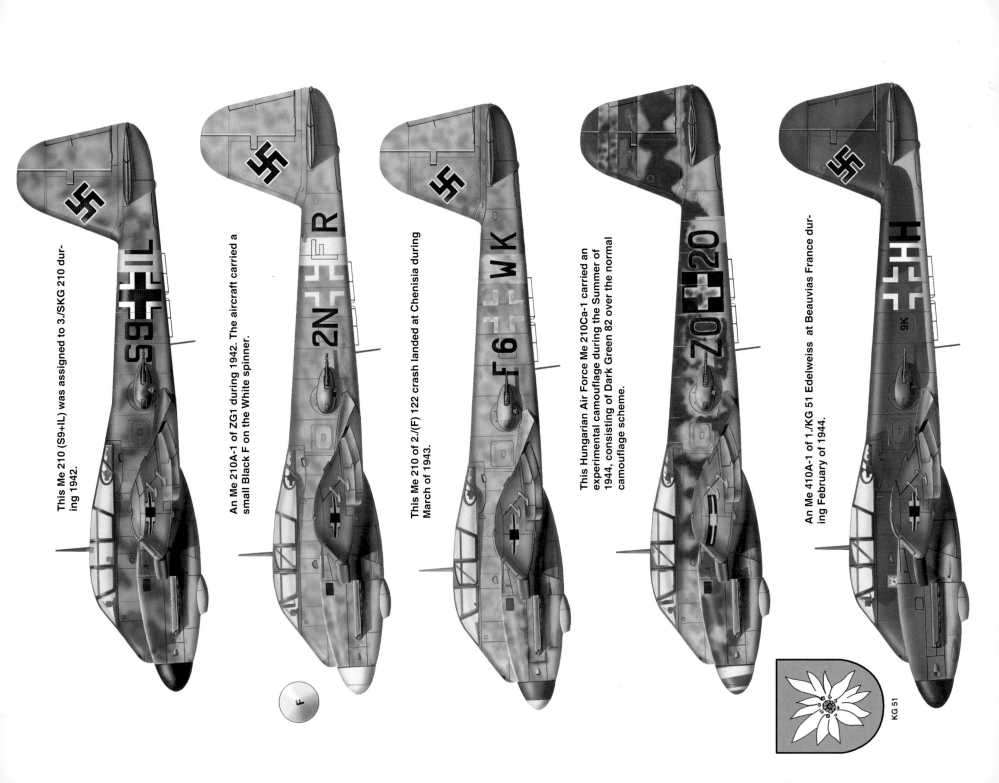

This Me 210 (S9+IL) was assigned to 3./SKG 210 during 1942.

An Me 210A-1 of ZG1 during 1942. The aircraft carried a small Black F on the White spinner.

This Me 210 of 2./(F) 122 crash landed at Chenisia during March of 1943.

This Hungarian Air Force Me 210Ca-1 carried an experimental camouflage during the Summer of 1944, consisting of Dark Green 82 over the normal camouflage scheme.

An Me 410A-1 of 1./KG 51 Edelweiss at Beauvias France during February of 1944.

KG 51

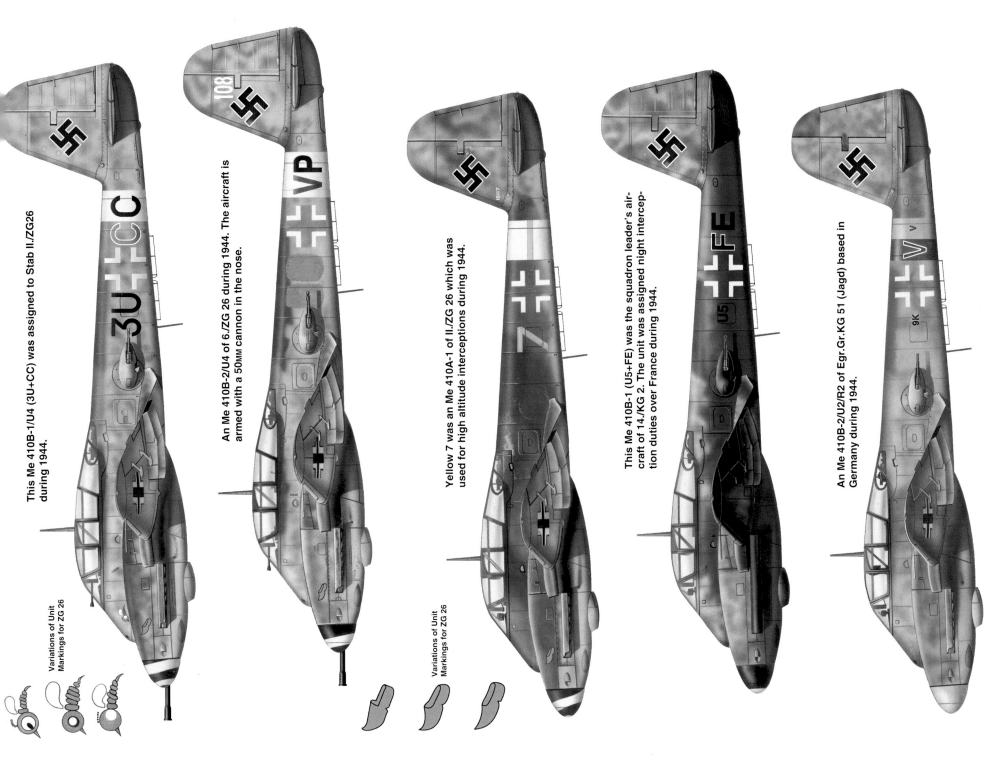

This Me 410B-1/U4 (3U+CC) was assigned to Stab II./ZG26 during 1944.

Variations of Unit Markings for ZG 26

An Me 410B-2/U4 of 6./ZG 26 during 1944. The aircraft is armed with a 50mm cannon in the nose.

Variations of Unit Markings for ZG 26

Yellow 7 was an Me 410A-1 of II./ZG 26 which was used for high altitude interceptions during 1944.

This Me 410B-1 (U5+FE) was the squadron leader's aircraft of 14./KG 2. The unit was assigned night interception duties over France during 1944.

An Me 410B-2/U2/R2 of Egr.Gr.KG 51 (Jagd) based in Germany during 1944.

This Me 210Ca-1 was used as an instructional aircraft at the mechanic's school in Ojvidek. The MG 151 cannon ports and MG-17 machine gun ports in the nose are both faired over. It is uncertain if this was a flyable aircraft, or merely a ground training airframe. (Kovács)

This Me 210Ca-1 was assigned to 102/2. Fast Bomber Squadron, based at Lesvar in northwest Hungary. The unit's Tiger insignia was painted on the fuselage side and there were several shell holes in the forward fuselage, wing flap and just under the gunner's cockpit. (Punka)

Ground crewmen perform maintenance on the 13MM MG 131 machine gun in the starboard turret. This aircraft has been over-sprayed with a darker color over its original Gray camouflage. The aircraft was assigned to 102/2. Fast Bomber Squadron at Lesvar the Winter of 1944. (Punka)

27

Me 410

Messerschmitt's next proposal was for a high altitude fighter/bomber with a pressurized cockpit and two 1,750 hp DB 603A engines. The armament was specified to be the same as that of the Me 210A-1. Various improvements were to have been incorporated, such as an increase in wing span to fifty-eight feet eight and three quarter inches and the installation of four blade propellers. The aircraft was anticipated to have a maximum speed of 419 mph at 36,090 feet. The thirteenth Me 210A-1(VN+AQ, Werk Nr. 2100179) was modified to this standard and flown on 11 September 1943. Two versions were proposed, the Me 310A-1 fast-bomber and the Me 310A-2 destroyer, but by the end of 1943, all further development of Me 310 was abandoned because it showed no major advantage over the Me 210.

The next design based on Me 210 was the Me 410 *Hornisse* (Hornet). The aircraft was essentially a Me 210A-1 with a lengthened fuselage, wing slats and re-engined with 1,750 hp DB 603A engines in a lengthened engine nacelle. The basic structure of the design remained the same as its predecessor, except that the taper of the outboard wing panels was reduced. This was due to the fact that the five degree sweep back used on the Me 210 wing was eliminated on the wing fitted with automatic leading edge slats. The geometry of the hydraulically operated camber-changing flaps was modified and the radiator flaps and the ailerons were also redesigned.

The Me 410V-1 prototype (DI+NW, Werk Nr. O27) was completed and flew near the end of 1942. After a series of successful tests using six modified Me 210As, the R.L.M. ordered the Me 410 into production. One of the modified Me 210s used in the test program was later supplied to Japan under the Nippon-German Technical Exchange Agreement. More than twenty *Versuchs* (experimental) aircraft were involved in the test program, mainly converted from Me 210 airframes, although a number were new-built aircraft.

The Me 410V-1 prototype (Werk Nr. O27) was originally built as an Me 210A-O. The aircraft was modified with DB 603A engines, lengthened rear fuselage and new wings during 1942. This aircraft was later assigned to III./ZG 1 as a Me 410A-1. (Dressel)

Me 410A Series

Production of the first variant, the Me 410A-1, began during January of 1943 and the first five aircraft were accepted by the Luftwaffe by the end of the month. The Me 410A-1 was a light bomber with the standard Me 210 armament of four machine guns and two cannons, plus various bomb loads in the internal bomb bay and on external bomb racks located under each wing root. Production priority was given to this variant, since the *Oberbefehlshaber der Luftwaffe* saw the *Schnellbomber* (fast bomber) role as the primary mission for the Me 410.

The Me 410A-1 was the basis for a number of conversions and factory kits were produced to allow conversion of the basic aircraft to perform a variety of missions. The Me 410A-1/U1 was a photo-reconnaissance modification with the two 7.9MM MG 17 machine guns being removed and replaced by a vertical camera, Rb (Reihenbild) 20/30, Rb 50/30 or Rb 75/30, in the modified bomb bay.

The Me 410A-1/U2 was a *Zerstörer* (destroyer) variant with provisions for an additional pair of 20MM MG 151/20 cannons with 250 rpg mounted in the bomb bay. The cannons were contained in a self-contained unit known as a *Waffenbehälter 151* (Weapons Container 151) which was loaded into the internal weapons bay of the Me 410 fully loaded with ammunition.

The Me 410A-1/U4 was a specialized bomber killer variant fitted with a 50MM BK 5 cannon and its twenty-one round cylindrical magazine in the internal weapons bay. The BK 5 cannon was first installed in the Me 410V-2 (originally Me 210A-0, CE+BZ, Werk Nr. 2100002). After completing all test flights and gun firing trials, the aircraft was delivered to *Erprobungskommando 25* for operational testing and evaluation. The aircraft was unarmed except for the BK 5 cannon. The later production variant retained its normal forward firing armament along with the installation of the heavy BK 5 cannon.

Fuselage Development

Me 210A-0

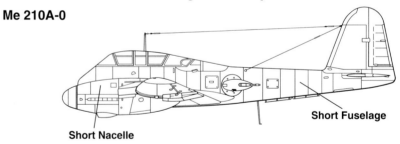

Short Nacelle

Short Fuselage

Me 410A-1

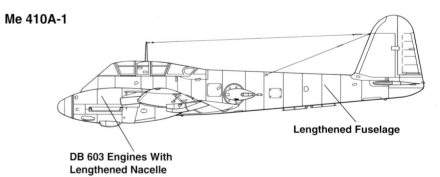

DB 603 Engines With Lengthened Nacelle

Lengthened Fuselage

The A-1 series used one of two different gun sights, either a Revi (*Reflexvisier*) C 12/D or ZFR (*Zielfernrohr*) ZFR 4A, later redesignated the Revi 16B. For bombing, the Me 410A-1 was equipped with a Stuvi 5B dive-bombing sight.

The second main production variant was the Me 410A-2, which was built primarily as a *Zerstörer*, with the two forward-firing MG 17 machine guns removed and replaced by two 30MM MK 103 cannons, which were installed in the bomb bay. It was built in a number of variations, mainly dealing with armament changes.

The Me 410A-2/U1 was similar to the Me 410A-1/U1 reconnaissance aircraft. The Me 410A-2/U2 was a night fighter modification fitted with radar antennas mounted on the nose. The Me 410A-2/U4 was similar to the A-1/U4, with a 50MM BK 5 cannon for bomber destroyer operations. Other armament options included various weapons kits that could be field installed on the Me 410.

Because of problems with the Me 410A-1/U1 and A-2/U1, a specialized reconnaissance variant was produced under the designation Me 410A-3. This variant mounted a pair of Rb 20/30, Rb 50/30 or Rb 75/30 cameras in the modified bomb bay. The modification of the bomb bay led to a deepened nose contour and both MG 17 machine guns were removed.

(Right) As they moved down the line, workmen installed different parts into the waiting airframes. These airframes have the main landing gear installed, some have engines, some have engines and cowlings, while the last two airframes have the wings. (Stapfer)

Workmen prepare a wing center section for mating to a Me 410 airframe, the round plates on the wing are service access panels.. The airframes in the background have their center sections in place along with the main landing gear. (Stapfer)

Workmen install cockpit parts to Me 410 airframes on the Messerschmitt Me 410 assembly line. The aircraft have the tail sections in place and the rudders were installed already painted. The aircraft at the end of the line have had their movable canopy sections installed. (Stapfer)

Engine Nacelle

Me 210A-1

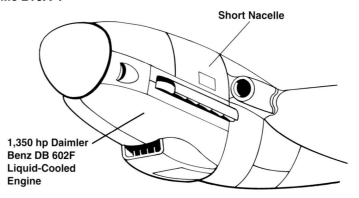

Short Nacelle

1,350 hp Daimler Benz DB 602F Liquid-Cooled Engine

This Me 410A-1/U2 (3U+MV, Werk Nr. 710340) of II./ZG 26 was fitted with underwing fuel tanks to allow it to provide cover for Fw 200s of KG 40 flying long range patrols from Norway. The fuselage band was Yellow and the aircraft carried a small M on the nose which was outlined in White. (Petrick)

This Me 410A-1(U5+KG, Werk Nr. 10185) of Stab V./KG 2 was fitted with flame damping tubes over the engine exhausts for use in the night fighting role. The individual aircraft letter, K, has a thin White outline. (Petrick)

Me 410A-1

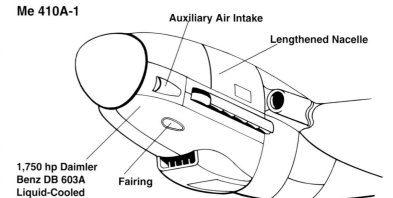

Auxiliary Air Intake

Lengthened Nacelle

1,750 hp Daimler Benz DB 603A Liquid-Cooled Engine

Fairing

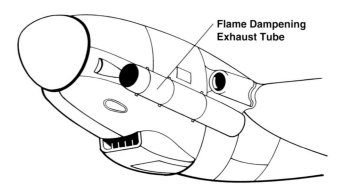

Flame Dampening Exhaust Tube

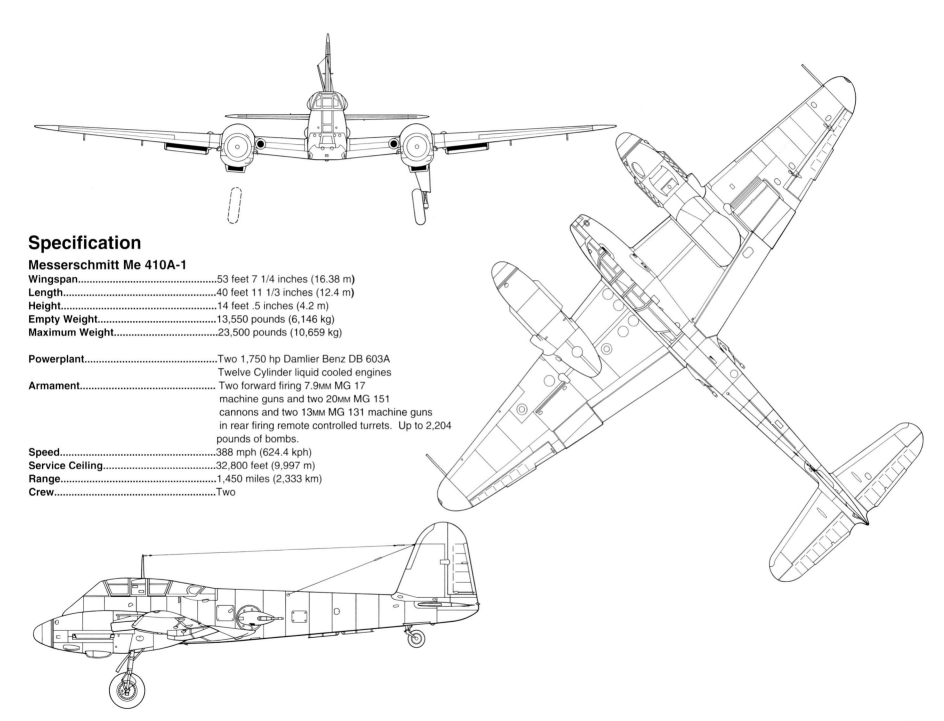

Specification

Messerschmitt Me 410A-1

Wingspan...53 feet 7 1/4 inches (16.38 m**)**
Length..40 feet 11 1/3 inches (12.4 m**)**
Height..14 feet .5 inches (4.2 m)
Empty Weight...13,550 pounds (6,146 kg)
Maximum Weight....................................23,500 pounds (10,659 kg)

Powerplant...Two 1,750 hp Damlier Benz DB 603A
Twelve Cylinder liquid cooled engines
Armament..Two forward firing 7.9ᴍᴍ MG 17
machine guns and two 20ᴍᴍ MG 151
cannons and two 13ᴍᴍ MG 131 machine guns
in rear firing remote controlled turrets. Up to 2,204
pounds of bombs.
Speed...388 mph (624.4 kph)
Service Ceiling.......................................32,800 feet (9,997 m)
Range...1,450 miles (2,333 km)
Crew...Two

A Me 410A-3 of 2./(F)122 taxies in to the waiting unit after completing the unit's 3,000th sortie. The Me 410A-3 had all forward firing armament removed and the ports faired over. The windows in the underside of the nose were camera ports. (Smithsonian)

Me 410A-1

7.9MM MG 17
Machine Gun Ports

20MM MG 151
Cannon Ports

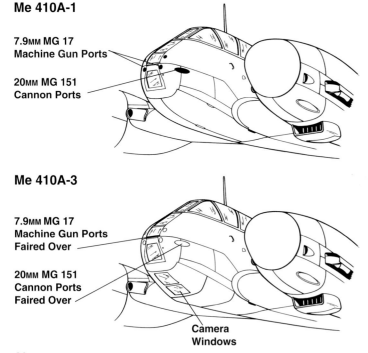

Me 410A-3

7.9MM MG 17
Machine Gun Ports
Faired Over

20MM MG 151
Cannon Ports
Faired Over

Camera
Windows

This Me 410A-1/U4 of V./KG 2 carried part of the Werk Number, 0012, on the nose in Black. This aircraft was declared missing in action on 30 July 1943, while being flown by *Oberleutnant* Biermann and his gunner *Underrldwebel* Krager. (Dressel)

Armament Modifications

Me 410A-1

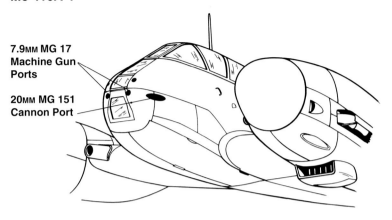

7.9MM MG 17 Machine Gun Ports

20MM MG 151 Cannon Port

Me 410A-2/U2

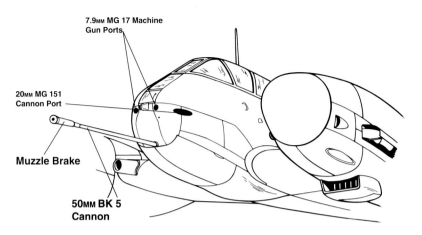

7.9MM MG 17 Machine Gun Ports

20MM MG 151 Cannon Port

Muzzle Brake

50MM BK 5 Cannon

Me 410A-2/R2

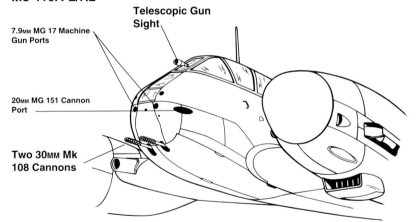

7.9MM MG 17 Machine Gun Ports

Telescopic Gun Sight

20MM MG 151 Cannon Port

Two 30MM Mk 108 Cannons

Factory Standard Mk 108 Muzzle Break

This Me 410A-1/U2 of ZG 101 was based at Memmingen during 1944. The aircraft's individual code number, 6, was repeated in White on the nose. The Me 410A-1/U2 was armed with an additional pair of 20MM MG 151 cannons in the under fuselage weapons bay. (Matthiesen)

Me 410B Series

In early 1944 the production tempo of the Me 410 was rapidly increasing and a new variant, the Me 410B was introduced. The Me 410B differed from the Me 410A series in that it was powered by 1,900 hp DB 603G engines in place of the 1,750 hp DB 603A engines used on the Me 410A. Additionally, the DB 603 was equipped with a higher speed supercharger.

The Me 410B-1 *Schnellbomber* was essentially the same as the Me 410A-1, with provision for two 79.25 gallon (300 liter) underwing fuel tanks, strengthened landing gear and with the nose mounted MG 17 machine guns being replaced by 13MM MG 131 weapons. The maximum bomb load (both internal and external) was 2,204 pounds (1,000 kg). The Me 410B was also equipped with a *Sturzkampfvisier Stuvi* 5B bomb sight.

The Me 410B-1/U2 was a *Zerstörer* with strengthened landing gear, a pair of nose-mounted 13MM MG 131 machine guns, two 20MM MG 151 cannons plus an WB(*Waffenbehälter*, weapons container)151A which held a pair of MG 151 cannons mounted in the bomb bay. The aircraft also had the provision for underwing fuel tanks.

The B-1/U4 was also a *Zerstörer* variant with the same modifications as the B-1/U2 but having the forward firing weapons replaced by a 50MM BK 5 cannon.

The B-2/U-2/R-2 had the two MG 17s removed from the nose and a pair of 30MM Mk 103 or Mk 108 cannons installed in the weapons bay. These mountings were known as *Rüstsatz* (Field Conversion Set) 2 or *Rüstsatz* 3. The *Rüstsatz* 2 comprised a *Waffenbehälter 105* (two 30MM Mk 108 cannons), The R3 was comprised a *Waffenbehälter 103* (two 30MM Mk 103 cannon and the R5 which consisted of four 20MM MG 151 in the *Waffenbehälter 151*.

The Me 410B-2/U-1 variant was similar to the B-1/U-1 with a WB (or WT-*Waffentropfen*, weapon drop) 151A installation with two 20MM MG 151 cannon. This was a bulged external container mounted under the central fuselage behind the bomb bay. The B-2/U2 carried four 20MM MG 151 cannon as standard armament.

The Me-410B2/U4 carried the 50MM Mk 5 cannon, like the earlier B-1/U4, but it also had a pair of 30MM cannons installed in the weapons bay. Some 100 conversion sets were produced by Messerschmitt to allow forward maintenance units to convert Me 410B-2s to the B-2/U-4 standard.

The next variant, the Me 410B-2/U-3 carried a FuG 200 *Hohentwiel* search radar with the two forward firing MG 131s being removed to make room for the radar installation. This aircraft had a single torpedo under the fuselage and a pair of 30MM cannons in the weapons bay.

Some other offensive weapons were tested for use in the Me 410 in the *Zerstörer* role, including the 37MM BK 3.7 cannon, which was installed in several machines in place of the standard 50MM BK 5 cannon.

The Me 410A-1 was tested with a rotating drum containing six launching tubes for 210MM rockets. The firing tests were begun on 3 February 1944 but the test was a complete failure and the airframe suffered extensive damage.

The Me 410B-3 was a reconnaissance variant with reduced forward firing armament (two MG 151) and two Rb 20/30,Rb 50/30 or Rb 75/30 cameras installed in the bomb bay.

The Me 410 B-5 was a torpedo-bomber variant with a FuG 200 *Hohentwiel* search radar and a pair of 20MM MG 151s in the nose. It carried a BT-Körper (Bomb-Torpedo Missiles) mounted on the port side of the fuselage undersurface. Other special weapons were tested for use on this variant including various torpedoes, glide bombs, the 2,205 pound (1,000 kg) SB 1000/410 thin-walled bomb which was stabilized during its fall by an automatically-operated

A Messerschmitt Me 410B-1/U2 (Werk Nr. 410096) of a training unit in Braunschweig-Waggum. This particular aircraft has no exhaust shrouds over the engine exhaust ports. The Me 410B-1/U-2 was armed with 13MM guns replacing the 7.9MM machine guns and an additional pair of 20MM cannons in the bomb bay. (Wiesinger via Obst. E. Peter)

parachute and the 1,720 pound (780 kg) SB 800 RS Kurt rolling bomb. Many of these weapons were tested on other Me 410s at the *Prüfplatz Leba, Pomerania* during 1944. Another weapon proposed for use on the Me 410B-5 was the L10 *Friedensengel* (peace angel) gliding torpedo. The *Friedensengel* was a miniature glider with a torpedo attached to it by a thirty-three foot cable. At the moment the glider made contact with the water, the torpedo was released from its carrier. For the aircraft to be used to its maximum range, the side gun turrets were removed and replaced by a 184 gallon fuel tank. Another auxiliary tank was also mounted in the weapons bay with all offensive loads being carried on the external racks. These could include either two BT 200 or BT 400 bomb-torpedoes, a single SC 1800 bomb beneath the fuselage or a 1,984 pound LT 5b or a 1,675 pound LT 5i torpedo.

The Me 410B-6 was built for anti-shipping reconnaissance duties with search radar, MG 131 machine guns replacing the MG 17s and an additional pair of 30MM Mk 103 cannons in a *Waffenbehälter 103* installation.

The Me 410B-7 and B-8 were projected reconnaissance variants for daylight and nocturnal operations, respectively. Both were to carry standard fighter armament, with the B-8 carrying flares in the bomb bay.

Several Me 410As were employed in the Me 410C and D projects. The Me 410C variant was to have featured DB 603JZ engines or (as alternatives) BMW 801TJ or Jumo 213 E/JZs. The project also featured a new wing of high aspect ratio and alternative outer wing panels which could increase the overall wing span from fifty-eight feet eleven inches to sixty-seven feet one inch. The fuselage nose was refined and the cockpit had a modified canopy. Unfortunately, the Me 410C prototype was never completed.

The Me 410D was proposed as night fighter variant with wooden outer wing panels (to conserve strategic materials) and the installation of *Lichtenstein C-1* or SN-2 air intercept radars.

The last proposed variant was the Me 410H, basically a Me 410B-2 powered by DB 603G engines and with an additional rectangular wing section inserted outboard of the engines. This increased the overall wing span to seventy-five feet five inches. Armament was intended to be two 20MM MG 151s, two 30MM Mk 103 and a pair of 30MM MK 108 in the nose. The bomb load was 2,205 pounds. The conversion of an Me 410B airframe was in progress at the end of the war, and like the earlier Me 410D, it was never completed.

Camouflage net drapes a Me 410B-1/U2/R4 destroyer as it was being prepared for its next mission from Konigsberg-Neumark during 1944. These heavily armed aircraft were ideal for engaging bomber formations, as long as there were no escort fighters in the area. (Petrick)

This Me 410B-1/U2 of ZG 1 carried WGR rocket tubes under the outer wing panels. Volleys of these were fired at American bomber formations, with the intent to break up the formations. Afterward, the Me 410s would pick off individual bombers with cannon fire. (Petrick)

This Me 410B-1 (Werk Nr. 425416) was experimentally fitted with a rotating launcher that contained six tubes for 210MM WGR rockets. The weapon was mounted in the modified bomb bay, and was tested on 3 February 1944 but the test was a complete failure and the airframe suffered extensive damage. (Nowarra)

A Me 410B-1/U2/R4 of 2./ZG 26 begins its takeoff role at Konigsberg-Neumark during the Summer of 1944. The unit number, 3U, was carried in small Black letters behind the fuselage band and the code letter, C, was Red with a thin White outline. (Petrick)

A Me 410B-2/U2/R5 destroyer with a WB 151A weapons container (four MG 151 20MM cannons) in the bomb bay. This aircraft has also been modified to carry an additional two 7.9MM MG 17s in the nose directly above the weapons bay. The port cabin air intake is closed. (Dressel)

Lieutenant Wenko starts the engines on his Me 410B-1/U2/R4 and prepares to depart on another interception mission against an American bomber formation. The aircraft carries a pair of 20MM MG 151 cannons in the bomb bay and a second pair in a pod under the fuselage. (Wiesinger via Wenko)

A pilot and gunner show off their Me 410B-2/U2/R5 to a friend. The aircraft was fitted with a WB 151A weapons container in the bomb bay (four 20MM MG 151 cannons). The upper MG 17s were removed from the nose on this aircraft and the exhaust shrouds are also missing. The small nose window was overpainted and the individual aircraft code letter, D, was carried on the nose in Red with a thin White outline. (Petrick)

Me 410B-2/U2s of I./ZG 26 were known as heavy destroyers. In addition to their battery of forward firing cannons, they were also fitted with four 210MM WGR rocket tubes, two under each wing. (Petrick)

Armament Options

Me 410B-2/U2/R4

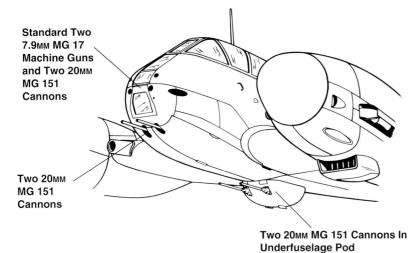

Standard Two 7.9MM MG 17 Machine Guns and Two 20MM MG 151 Cannons

Two 20MM MG 151 Cannons

Two 20MM MG 151 Cannons In Underfuselage Pod

Me 410B-2/U2/R5

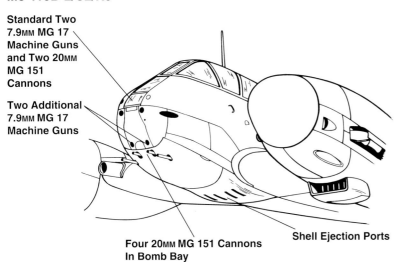

Standard Two 7.9MM MG 17 Machine Guns and Two 20MM MG 151 Cannons

Two Additional 7.9MM MG 17 Machine Guns

Four 20MM MG 151 Cannons In Bomb Bay

Shell Ejection Ports

A Me 410B-1/U2 outfitted with a R4 container (two MG 151 20MM cannons) under the fuselage on the airfield at Konigsberg-Neumark during the Summer of 1944. The aircraft has the individual aircraft number, 6, on the nose in Black with a thin White outline. (Petrick)

Four Me 410B-2/U-4s (3U+MP, 3U+CP, 3U+VP and 3U+LP) of 6./ZG 26 are starting their takeoff roll on another interception mission. The individual identification letter on each aircraft was in red. Two of the aircraft carry three digits of the Werk Number on the vertical stabilizer in White. (Petrick)

The three White stripes around the BK 5 cannon barrel of this Me 410B-2/U-4 are victory stripes. The aircraft's pilot, Lieutenant Frös of 2./ZG 26, shot down three Boeing B-17s during April of 1944. (Petrick)

The barrel of the 50mm BK 5 cannon extended a considerable distance in front of the nose. These Me 410B-2/U4 crewmen are waiting for the next scramble at Konigsberg during the Autumn of 1944. The cone sticking out of the windshield is a telescopic gun sight. (Petrick)

Me 410B-2/U-4

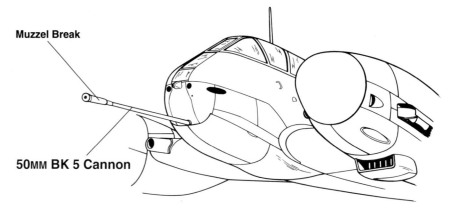

Muzzel Break

50mm BK 5 Cannon

This Me 410B-2/U-4 armed with a 50MM BK-5 cannon was captured and evaluated by the Soviets. The aircraft was tested at Ramenskoye airfield in Moscow during 1945 and was only partially repainted with Soviet insignia. (Gretzyngier)

This Me 410 of II./ZG 26 was armed with four WGR 210MM underwing rocket tubes (two under each outer wing panel). The Holzschuh unit insignia is just visible on the engine cowling just above the rocket tube. (Petrick)

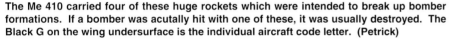

The Me 410 carried four of these huge rockets which were intended to break up bomber formations. If a bomber was acutally hit with one of these, it was usually destroyed. The Black G on the wing undersurface is the individual aircraft code letter. (Petrick)

WGR Rocket Tubes

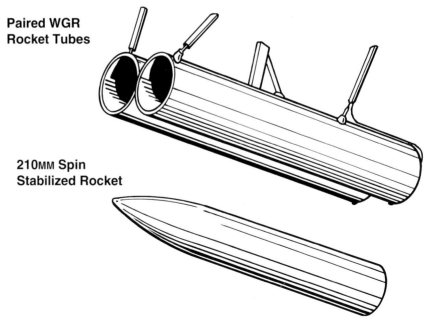

Paired WGR Rocket Tubes

210MM Spin Stabilized Rocket

Me 410 In Service

The first five production Me 410s were accepted by the Luftwaffe in January of 1943 and by the end of April, some forty-eight aircraft had been delivered.

During April and May of 1943, the Me 210 aircraft of II/ZG 1 *Wespen* and 2/.(F)122 were replaced by Me 410A-1/U2s. One of the first Reich Zerstörer (destroyer) units to re-equipped with the new type, was *Erprobungskommando 25*, commanded by *Hauptmann* (Captain) Eduard Tratt in Wittmundhafen. This was a special unit formed to conduct operational tests of new weapons, heavy cannons and rockets.

In September of 1943, *Hauptmann* Tratt left *Erprobungskommando 25* and took over command of II/ZG 26 *Horst Wessel*. This fighter group began operations against the Americans as a Home Defense unit based at Oberpfaffenhofen and later Königsberg (Tratt died on 22 February 1944 in an engagement against American four-engined bombers near Nordhausen). At the time of his death, he was an ace with thirty-eight kills.

5./KG 2 had begun conversion from the Do 217 to the Me 410A-1 during April of 1943. Before conversion was complete, the entire *Gruppe* went back to Do 217s and transferred their Me 410s to V./KG 2. This *Gruppe* was to take part, under the command of *Angriffsführer England*, in "Baby Blitz" operations over the British Isles during 1943-44. In January of 1944, V./KG 2 was redesignated as II./KG 51 and, together with I./KG 51 *Edelweiss* and the *Geschwader Stab*, began operations under the control of the *Luftwaffenbefehlshaber Mitte* in France. The unit achieved operational status at Beauvais during 1944.

On 2 April 1944, about fifteen Me 410s of KG 51 followed the bombers of the USAAF's 2nd Division back to their home bases in England. Shortly after the bombers landed, the German force attacked, destroying a number of B-24s for the loss of one Me 410 to anti-aircraft fire. This aircraft (9K+HP, Werk Nr. 420458) was seen to explode over Ashby, killing the pilot, *Oberleutnant* (1st Lieutenant) Klaus Krüger and his radio-operator *Felbwebel* (Sergeant) Reichardt.

By the end of 1943, the Augsburg assembly line had delivered some 457 Me 410As to Luftwaffe units. The first Dornier-built aircraft was accepted in December, but the next eleven were not delivered until the following February.

The first operational casualty for V./KG 2 was U5+KG, which was shot down on the night of 13-14 July 1943, by a Mosquito NF XII of No 85 Squadron near Felixstowe, with *Feldwebel* (Sergeant) Zwissler at the controls and *Oberfelbwebel* (Master Sergeant) Raida flying as radio-operator/gunner. Another Me 410 (U5+CJ) of V. *Gruppe, Kampfgeschwader 2* also was downed by a night fighter Mosquito near Dunkirk.

During early 1943, American attacks against targets in the Third Reich had not been significant, because they had been few and far between and of an experimental nature. Additionally, these raids were modest in scale, involving only a few aircraft. By the Summer of 1943, all this had changed and the raids increased in their effectiveness.

As a result, the Luftwaffe was forced to pull back more and more fighters from other fronts to form *Reichsverteidigung* (home defense) units. The twin-engined *Zerstörers* were best suited for these units since they had the range to enable them to fight the long air battles with the four-engined bombers and had heavier armament than the early single-engined fighter types in service.

During September of 1943 II./ZG 26 *Horst Wessel* began to replace its Me 210s with Me 410A-2/U4s. After re-equipping with the new aircraft, the *Gruppe* operated with the another great *Horniss*e unit, ZG 76, against the 8th Army Air Force over Germany, Austria, Hungary

The crew of this Me 410A (Werk Nr. 420090) jettisoned the canopy before making a belly landing at Gotenhafen/Hexengrund on 4 October 1944. From the condition of the propeller, the engines were still running at the time of impact. (Griehl)

The crew of this Me 410A-3 has just landed after completing the unit's 3,000 sortie. Such celebrations were a common practice in the Luftwaffe. The small blister on the canopy is the bubble over the Revi gunsight. (Smithsonian)

A mechanic works on the starboard engine of an Me 410B-2/U2/R2 (RN+Z) during the summer of 1944. In addition to its standard armament, the aircraft carries two additional MG 151 20MM cannon in the weapons bay. (Radinger)

A pair of Me 410B-1/U2/R4 (3U+GK and 3U+CK) of 2./ZG 26 formate over Bremen after a sortie against an 8th Air Force bomber raid on 8 October 1943. These aircraft carry the unit number (3U) in small Black letters to the rear of the fuselage band. (Petrick)

A pair of Me 410s (9K+Vv and 9K+Ww) of *Erg. Gruppe KG 51(Jagd)*. It was the practice of this unit to carry the individual aircraft letter in Red with a thin White outline. The letter was carried twice, once in a large size and then repeated in a much small size. These aircraft also carry the Red/Yellow Reich Defense band around the fuselage. (Archives Lorant via Kruse)

and Czechoslovakia.

On 16 March 1944, a force of Bf 110s and Me 410s attacked about 500 B-17 Fortresses and 200 B-24 Liberators of the 8th Air Force that were attacking the aircraft factories in South-Germany. The bombers were hit by *Zerstörer* units firing rockets and heavy cannons with some eighteen B-17s and B-24s being shot down. The *Zerstörers* waited for the moment when the short ranged escort fighters were forced to turn back by a lack of fuel, then they attacked. These tactics resulted in heavy American losses.

In April, the 8th Air Force attacked again aiming to destroy additional German aircraft production centers. On 10 April more than 900 B-17s and B-24s were sent to six targets in Eastern Germany, escorted by six P-51 Mustang and four P-38 Lightning fighter groups. Between Poznan and Rostock, the 45th and the 13th Bomber Wings were attacked by Ju 88s and rocket-firing Me 410s. The *Zerstörer* units destroyed a total of twenty-five bombers. The unescorted 40th Bomb Wing over Stettin was hit by rocket and cannon firing *Zerstörers* of ZG 26, with heavy losses. The total losses for the 8th Air Force was fifty-two B-17s, twelve B-24s and sixteen fighters.

On 7 July 1944, over Halle and Bernburg, Me 410s and Fw 190s attacked B-24 Liberators flying against oil refineries and aircraft factories in the Reich. Two P-38 Lightning Groups claimed seven Me 410s destroyed for the loss of one P-38. Captain James Morris, the 20th Group's leading ace with seven and a half kills was shot down by the side 13MM guns of a Me 410 which he was attacking. The 38th Fighter Squadron engaged a score of the Me 410s and in a matter of minutes had shot down three and damaged four.

Located in Austria, Hungary and Czechoslovakia were the last oil refineries of the Reich, which were mostly undamaged during 1944. These targets came under attack by the 15th U.S. Army Air Force flying from bases in Italy.

On 16 June 1944, the 376th Bomb Group led an attack against the Nova Oil Refinery at Schwechat near Vienna and the Apollo Refinery at Pozsony (Bratislava), Czechoslovakia.

Aircrews push the BMW Cabriolet of *Oblt.* Guth past a pair of Me 410s of Stab I./ZG 26. The aircraft in the background has the individual aircraft letter, A, in Green. It was flown by Lieutenant Wenko. (Wiesinger via Wenko)

Oberleutnant Jenne, *Gruppenkommander* of I./ZG 26 in the cockpit of his Me 410. The front armored glass panel has been removed and the Revi gunsight is visible under the small bubble in the windshield. There is a small mirror mounted on the canopy framing (just to the left of the pilot's head). (Wiesinger via Wenko)

Over the target area some forty single and twin-engined fighters and destroyers attacked the bomber boxes from all angles. During the fighting, Liberator gunners scored several victories. One Me 410A-1 of I./ZG 76 was shot down four miles from Gönyü, Hungary with both crew men being killed. Another *Hornisse*, a Me 410B-2 of II./ZG 76, was brought down twelve miles west Gyõr (Raab), Hungary.

The targets for the bombers on 26 June were the five oil refineries near Vienna. Over Moosbierbaum, a formation of thirty-six B-24s of the 455th Bomb Group were attacked by more than twenty twin-engined *Zerstörers* of I./ZG 76, while several single-engined fighters were engaged by the escort. The Me 410s attacked the B-24s with rockets and cannon fire. During this action, the bomber gunners shot down a number of Me 410s including M8+1 (Werk Nr. 120101) which was lost over Alsokemenes in Hungary, with its crew, pilot Straube and gunner Schroer, being killed in action. Another Me 410B-2/U2 (M8+9, Werk Nr. 470130) went down near Kuty in Bohemia-Moravia with her crew *Gefreiter* Evers and *Gefreiter* Schauenburg. Over Koniggratz, northeast of Prague, a third Me 410 was lost, M8+15 (Werk Nr. 120015) again the crew, pilot Besemüller and his gunner, Wassermann, were killed.

Two weeks later, on 8 July, the Florisdorf oil refinery was bombed by the 55th Bomb Wing. For twenty-five minutes after the bombers left the target, they came under heavy attack by sixty German fighters and destroyers. In the battle, the 464th Bomb Group lost three aircraft and the 465th Bomb Group lost one Liberator, but its gunners claimed several fighters. The three squadrons of I./ZG 76 lost eight Me 410A-1s, Me 410A-1/U2s, Me 410B-l/U2s and Me 410B-2/U2s.

External Bomb Racks

Me 210Ca-1 and Me 410A-1

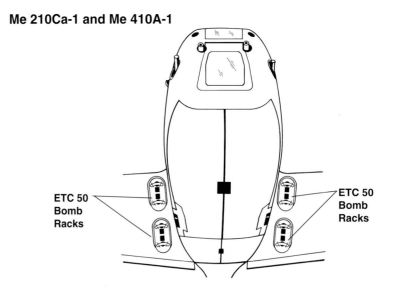

ETC 50 Bomb Racks

ETC 50 Bomb Racks

Lieutenant Hannes Wenko and his mechanic just before take off on another intercept mission. The Me 410B-1/U4/R4 had a piece of armor glass mounted behind the seat armor for added protection from rear attacks. (Wiesinger via Wenko)

This Me 410B-1/U2 of ZG 26 made a crash landing at Konigsberg-Neumark during 1944. The aircraft carries a White A2 marking on the starboard engine nacelle and has had the two nose mounted MG 17s removed and the ports faired over. (Petrick)

The squadron insignia was carried on the starboard Daimler Benz engine nacelle of this Me 410 of I./ZG 26. The aircraft's spinner was Black with a Yellow spiral. The officer in the middle is Major Hans Kogler *Geschwaderkommodore* of ZG 26. (Wiesinger via Wenko)

43

After mid-July of 1944, the twin-engined Me 410 destroyers were noticeably absent, since ZG 26 and ZG 76 were being disbanded. Since the steady increase in Allied fighter units, there was no longer a safe area within Germany where destroyers could be employed without unacceptable risks. The production of single-engined fighters became a priority and the bombing of factories and depots had also brought a maintenance and spare-parts problem. The decision was taken to withdraw the Me 410s from combat. From September of 1944 on, production of Me 410s was phased out with a total of 702 Me 410s having been delivered to Luftwaffe units when production ended. By the end of 1944, apart from IV./ZG 26, based in Norway, the only remaining Me 410s in service were flown strictly in the reconnaissance role.

Luftwaffe units equipped with Messerschmitt Me 410s, 1943-45: *V./KG 2* (U5+), *I., II., III./KG 51* (9K+), *Ergänzungskommando 25*, *Ergänzungskommando 410*, *1./(F)122* (F6+), *2./(F)122* (F6+), *5./(F)122* (F6+), *Erg. Fernaufklarer Gruppe* (F2+, only a few aircraft for training purposes), *I. II. III./ ZG 1* (2N+), *I.II./ZG 26* (3U+), *I., II./ZG 76* (M8+), *1./(F)121* (7A+), *Erg. Zerstarergruppe* (1E+), *Seenot Gruppe 80* (F4+), *Seenot Gruppe 60*, *Seenot Gruppe 81*, *I./Schlachtgeschwader 152* (4M+) and *IV./ZG 26* (4A+)

This Me 410A-1(Werk Nr. 10117) on the ramp at Hildesheim during 1944, has the 13MM gun barbettes and cockpit canopy radio mast deleted. The Yellow number, 7, and horizontal bar marking identify this aircraft as belonging to *II. Gruppe*. (Petrick)

An Me 410B-2/R2 (M8+2) of I./ZG 76 on a German base in Czechoslovakia during late 1944. The aircraft is fitted with a non-standard flame damper over the exhausts. The squadron code, M8, is carried in small Black letters just in front of the individual aircraft number. (Chapmann)

A pair of Me 410B-2/R2s of II./ZG 76 parked on a field in southern Czechoslovakia during 1944. The aircraft was armed with a pair of Mk 103 cannons mounted in the bomb bay and were fitted with telescopic gunsights which protrude from the windscreen. The aircraft in the background has a Red Reich Defense fuselage band and a horizontal stripe which identifies it as being assigned to *II.Gruppe*. (Chapmann)

Aircrews walk out to their waiting Me 410B-1/U4s of Stab II./ZG 26 at Konigsberg during the Autumn of 1944. These aircraft are armed with 37MM BK 39 cannons mounted in the bomb bays and have telescopic gunsights. The outlined letter on the fuselage was in Green. (Petrick)

(Right) Aircraft of 4./ZG 26 crowd the airfield at Konigsberg-Neumark during late 1944. The individual letters on these aircraft are in White and the unit code is in small Black letters on the fuselage band. The aircraft in the background has an unusual camouflage and the hangar has a full size front view illustration of a B-17 painted on it. (Petrick)

A Me 410B-6/R2 of *Seenot Gruppe 81*. This aircraft carried an FuG 200 surface search radar, with the antenna array mounted on the nose. (International War Museum)

Oblt. Abrahamczik (middle) in front of his Me 410B-1 (U5+FE) in France during February of 1944. He was the squadron leader of 14./KG 2 and had the undersurfaces of his aircraft painted Black for night operations. (Petrick)

Radar Variants

Me 210A-1

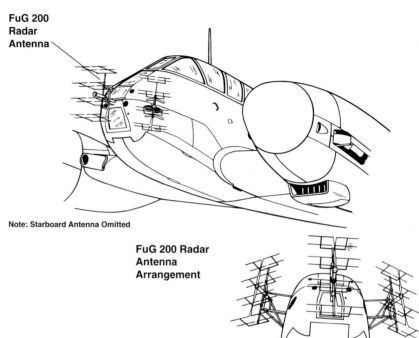

FuG 200 Radar Antenna

Note: Starboard Antenna Omitted

FuG 200 Radar Antenna Arrangement

Me 410B-6/R-2

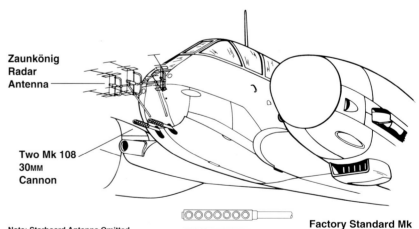

Zaunkönig Radar Antenna

Two Mk 108 30MM Cannon

Factory Standard Mk 108 Muzzle Break

Note: Starboard Antenna Omitted

During the later months of the war a number of Me 410B-3s of 2./(F)122 were stationed Kastrup. These reconnaissance aircraft carried no armament in the nose, all normal weapons having been deleted. (Petrick)

A badly damaged, unarmed, Me 410B-3 reconnaissance aircraft of an unidentified reconnaissance unit rests on an airfield in East Prussia at the end of the war. These aircraft were some of the last Me 410s to remain active. (Kulikov)

Ground crewmen service a Me 410B-1 (TF+EQ) stationed in Le Mans, France. The aircraft was part of *Stab/3.Jagd-Division*. The covers over the 13MM side gun mounts have been removed so that the guns can be serviced and reloaded. (Dressel)

A Me 410B-1/U2/R4 destroyer undergoes servicing before another mission from Konigsberg-Neumark during 1944. Within a few short months the Me 410 would be pulled from service. (Petrick)

A pair of Me 410B-2/U2s (F4+CC and F4+HC) of *Seenot Gruppe 80* rest on the airfield at Westerland-Sylt during 1945 with their propellers removed to prevent them from being flown. (Newark Air Museum)

After the German surrender, large numbers of Luftwaffe aircraft were captured intact. This Me 410A-1/U2 (F6+AN) of 5./FAGr.122 was found in Beldringe minus its propellers and empty of fuel during May of 1945. (Royal Danish Air Force)

This Me 210A-1 (SI+KN, Werk Nr. 271) and a number of engines were found in Bindbach, near Bayreuth by American troops during May of 1945. The aircraft has had its Luftwaffe insignia overpainted in preparation for shipment. (USAF)

Me 410s along with many other aircraft types rest in a Luftwaffe aircraft graveyard in Germany during 1945. Toward the end of the war, large numbers of aircraft were abandoned due to fuel shortages, most of these were later dumped in these graveyards. (Dressel)

(Above & Below) American troops captured this Me 410A-3 (ex F6+WK) of 2./(F)122. It was returned to the United States and put on exhibit with other captured aircraft. The FE code on the aircraft was a USAAF identification number. The aircraft carried the spinner from a Focke Wulf 190 on the starboard engine, probably a replacement. (Dressel)

Luftwaffe Aircraft

From

squadron/signal publications

1073

Ju 87 Stuka
in action

SPECIAL 8 EXTRA PAGES

squadron/signal publications
AIRCRAFT NO. 73

1044

Messerschmitt Bf 109
in action
Part 1

squadron/signal publications
AIRCRAFT No. 44

1057

Messerschmitt Bf 109
in action
Part 2

SPECIAL 8 EXTRA PAGES

Aircraft Number 57
squadron/signal publications

1085

Junkers Ju 88
in action
Part 1

squadron/signal publications, inc.   Aircraft Number 85

SPECIAL 8 EXTRA PAGES

1113

Junkers Ju 88
in action
Part 2

Aircraft Number 113
squadron/signal publications

SPECIAL 8 EXTRA PAGES

1142

FOCKE-WULF Fw 189
in action

Aircraft Number 142
squadron/signal publications